Haunted Houses

by Grace Hansen

Abdo Kids Jumbo is an Imprint of Abdo Kids
abdopublishing.com

abdopublishing.com

Published by Abdo Kids, a division of ABDO, P.O. Box 398166, Minneapolis, Minnesota 55439.
Copyright © 2019 by Abdo Consulting Group, Inc. International copyrights reserved in all countries.
No part of this book may be reproduced in any form without written permission from the publisher.
Abdo Kids Jumbo™ is a trademark and logo of Abdo Kids.

052018

092018

THIS BOOK CONTAINS
RECYCLED MATERIALS

Photo Credits: Alamy, Granger Collection, iStock, Shutterstock, ©Gillett's Crossing p.11/CC BY 2.0
©Justin Cheung p.15/CC BY-ND 2.0

Production Contributors: Teddy Borth, Jennie Forsberg, Grace Hansen

Design Contributors: Dorothy Toth, Laura Mitchell

Library of Congress Control Number: 2017960577

Publisher's Cataloging-in-Publication Data

Names: Hansen, Grace, author.

Title: Haunted houses / by Grace Hansen.

Description: Minneapolis, Minnesota : Abdo Kids, 2019. | Series: Amusement park rides |
    Includes glossary, index and online resources (page 24).

Identifiers: ISBN 9781532108020 (lib.bdg.) | ISBN 9781532109003 (ebook) |
    ISBN 9781532109492 (Read-to-me ebook)

Subjects: LCSH: Haunted houses (Amusements)--Juvenile literature. | Amusement rides--Juvenile
    literature. | Amusement parks--Juvenile literature.

Classification: DDC 791.068--dc23

Table of Contents

First Frights

Some people think being scared is fun! People have told each other spooky stories for centuries. It is a form of entertainment.

Haunted houses often have creepy characters, dark rooms, and **eerie** music. Going through a haunted house is like living your own scary story.

In 1802, Marie Tussaud made headless wax figures. She housed them in London in a place she called the "Chamber of Horrors." People loved to visit it.

9

The first recorded haunted mansion opened in 1915 in the United Kingdom. It was called the Orton and Spooner Ghost House.

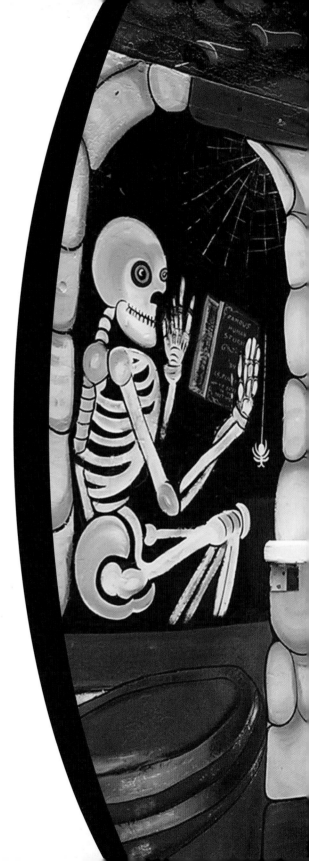

11

The first haunted houses came to the United States in the 1930s. Parents decorated their homes on Halloween. It kept kids from playing bad tricks.

13

Disney & Hollywood

Disneyland's Haunted Mansion opened in 1969. Walt Disney always dreamed of creating one. And his was perfect!

14

Haunted houses quickly spread throughout the country. People flocked to them to be spooked!

Hollywood had many scary movies in the 1980s and 1990s. Favorite characters, like Ghostface from *Scream*, popped up in haunted houses.

New Ideas

Escape Rooms are a new kind of haunted house. People locked inside work together to solve puzzles and riddles. Then they are freed!

More Facts

- People were very excited about Disney's haunted mansion. Soon after it opened, more than 82,000 people went through it in one day.

- In the Halloween season, a professional haunted house can earn around $3 million.

- Fear causes the brain to trigger an **adrenaline** release. Those who go to haunted houses know they are safe. So fear becomes fun!

Glossary

adrenaline – a hormone made by the body that makes your heart beat faster and prepares you to react to danger.

century – a unit of time equal to 100 years.

eerie - mysterious and frightening.

Index

Abdo Kids
ONLINE
FREE! ONLINE MULTIMEDIA RESOURCES

Visit **abdokids.com** and
use this code to access crafts,
games, videos, and more!

Abdo Kids Code:
AHK8020